500017795716

CW01476480

STOP BULLYING ME!

Written by Jenny Powell
Illustrated by Sophie Keen

WAYLAND

Stop Bullying Me! can be used during Shared or Guided Reading sessions with individuals or small groups of children. It can also be performed by the whole class with named parts given to individual children and the rest of the class playing the parts of the extras.

This play can also be used as part of anti-bullying week, as a PSHME focus within the classroom, as part of the Year 4 Literacy unit 4 'Stories which Raise Issues/Dilemmas' or within unit 5 about 'Plays'.

Sets and props

Creating the sets and finding the props for your play can be as much fun as putting on the performance!

You could tape together some white paper to make some large backdrops for the scenes and paint them to create the sets; you will need a backdrop for the school, Harry's home and the outside of Louis' house.

You can perform the play without having to find lots of different props. The books, pencils and notepads you need in the classroom scenes can be your own. The family's kitchen table could be made from three classroom tables. These could then be separated and used as desks in the classroom and then reassembled to form Ms Newton's desk and the tables in the dining hall.

Staging

There is no need to put on a huge production. All you need in order to perform the play is a large enough space for a stage and room for an audience to watch the performance. If you have access to an outside space and the weather is good, you can even put on the play in the open air!

Costumes

Costumes can also be kept simple and you can have great fun coming up with ideas of costumes for each character.

The children in the play could wear shirts and trousers or even their own school uniform to play Harry, Louis and his gang. Mr Jackson could have a beard made from string and cotton wool and Ms Newton could wear a pair of glasses.

HAVE FUN PUTTING ON YOUR PLAY!

Go to www.waylandbooks.co.uk for more ideas.

Foreward from Kidscape

Bullying affects thousands of children every day. It is never acceptable, as regardless of the circumstances there are no excuses. No one has the right to bully another person. **Stop Bullying Me!** illustrates the rejection and social exclusion experienced by targets of peer-led aggression. This dynamic play gives children several clear messages. Importantly, they learn that bullying is always wrong, that bullies have to take responsibility for the hurt they cause others and that targets must not keep bullying a secret. This very effective teaching tool also highlights the importance of friendship, which provides the best protection against bullying. Children will enjoy performing the play and will be left with a heightened awareness of the consequences of being cruel to others.

Claude Knights, Director of Kidscape

Introduction

This play is set in a modern day school and explores issues surrounding verbal bullying and loneliness. The scenes are set in the school, at Harry's home and at the bully's home.

The characters in the play

 ● **Harry**

 ● **Millie**
Harry's little
sister

 ● **Mum**

 ● **Dad**

 ● **Louis**

 ● **Lily**

 ● **Faisal**

 ● **Alfie**

 ● **Ms Newton**
Harry's teacher

 ● **Mrs Hastings**
Louis' Mum

 ● **Mr Jackson**

 ● **Narrator**

● **Extras:** children in the school and class

CHARACTERS IN THIS SCENE:

● Narrator ● Harry ● Mum ● Dad ● Millie

*It's a Monday evening and **Harry**'s family are sitting around the dinner table, eating tea.*

● **Harry:** (*excitedly*) Did you know that a polar bear is the world's largest land predator? Isn't that amazing? And also a polar bear cannot see anything until it is one month old! Oh and another thing…

● **Millie:** (*sighing*) Give it a rest Harry. I know you've loved learning about polar bears today at school, but do we have to hear about them all night? Is there nothing else you have to say?

● **Mum:** I agree, let's talk about something else! How was your day, Millie?

● **Harry:** But, Mum — I have so much more to tell you.

● **Dad:** Tell us later, Harry. Let your sister tell us about her day now.

● **Narrator:** Harry loves to learn new things. He adores going to school and wants to learn as much as he can. But things are about to change for Harry…

SCENE 2

CHARACTERS IN THIS SCENE:

- **Narrator** • **Harry** • **Ms Newton** • **Louis**
- **Lily** • **Extras** – *children in the class*

*It is Tuesday morning. **Harry** is at school, sitting in his classroom. A maths lesson is taking place.*

● **Narrator:** It is Tuesday morning and Harry is excited about the idea of learning new things at school. But there is a new boy who has started at Harry's school today and he is in Harry's class.

*Enter **Ms Newton** and **Louis**.*

● **Ms Newton:** Good morning children. This is Louis. (*points to **Louis***) It is his first day here and he will be joining our class. I know you will all make Louis feel welcome at our school. Please show him around, ask him to play with you and help him settle in. Louis, why don't you take a seat over there? (*Points to **Harry**'s table.*)

8

Ms Newton: Right, here is a challenging maths question to wake your brains up this morning. There are some goats and ducks near a pond. They have 40 heads and 88 feet between them. How many goats are there? How many ducks are there?

40 heads + 88 feet
= ?? goats
?? ducks

Pause whilst the class work out the maths puzzle.
*All the **children** are scribbling in their books.*

● **Harry:** *(putting his hand up)* I know, I know, Ms Newton, there are lots of ways to solve it but one way could be that there are 16 goats and 12 ducks. Is that right?

Ms Newton: Excellent, Harry, you solved that very quickly – and yes that is one possible answer. Has anyone got another suggestion?

Louis: (*whispering to* **Lily**) What a loser! I'm going to hate it here if everyone is like that kid.

Lily: Don't worry, Louis, he's the only freak in our class. The rest of us are normal. As if anyone could work out the answer to that question. (*Glares at* **Harry**.)

Narrator: Louis and Lily do not love to learn and Louis instantly takes a dislike to Harry, who seems to find the lesson so easy.

Louis: So, what do you do with kids like Harry at this school? (*pointing to* **Harry**) Someone needs to deal with losers like that.

Lily: (*nodding*) It's about time Harry understood what a nerd he is. Have you got any ideas then, Louis?

Louis: (*grinning*) Get your friends together at lunchtime. I'll show you what we can do!

The **children** *leave the classroom as the bell rings to signal the end of the lesson.*

CHARACTERS IN THIS SCENE:

● Narrator ● Harry ● Louis ● Faisal ● Alfie
● Lily ● Extras – *children in the playground*

Harry is sitting, reading his book in the playground. The gang approach him, with **Louis** at the front. There are other **children** eating and chatting at tables and sitting on the grass.

● **Louis:** Hey! You! (*shouts at* **Harry**)
Moron, don't you have anything better to
do than read a book? How boring are you?

● **Faisal:** Yeah – don't you have any friends,
you nerd?

● **Harry:** I'm not a nerd!

● **Alfie:** You're a nerd, you can't even find anyone
to play with at lunchtime. The only thing you can
do is read a book.

The gang are now surrounding **Harry***.*

● **Lily:** I'll have that. (*She snatches the book
out of* **Harry***'s hand and begins to rip out the pages.*)

● **Harry:** Hey, that's mine! (*Tries to grab the book back.*)

● **Louis:** Hang on a minute, Lily. The fact that he is a complete
loser could actually help us…

● **Lily:** (*puzzled*) What do you mean, Louis?

● **Louis**: (*pausing and thinking*) Right, here's the deal, Harry.
If you help me and my new friends here with our maths homework,
we won't tell anyone how you still wet the bed.

● **Harry**: (*scared and confused*) But I don't wet the bed…

● **Louis:** Do you think I care? If I tell everyone that you do, they'll believe me. I'm going to be one of the coolest kids at this school. People will believe whatever I say.

● **Faisal:** And they'll listen to me. I'm the best footballer here, everyone listens to what I have to say.

● **Alfie:** If you don't help us, Louis will make your life horrible. Trust me!

● **Harry:** OK, I'll do your homework. Just *(shouts)* LEAVE ME ALONE!

● **Extras:** Loser, loser, loser, loser!

Louis *and the gang leave looking very smug.*

● **Narrator:** Harry is confused and is very upset. No one has ever said or done such unkind things to him before.

The bell rings and all ***children*** *go back into school.*
Harry slowly walks back into class with his head down.

SCENE 4

CHARACTERS IN THIS SCENE:

● Narrator ● Harry ● Louis ● Mr Jackson ● Lily
● Faisal ● Alfie ● Extras – *other children in dining hall*

*Harry decides to tell someone about the bullying.
One lunchtime, he goes to speak to **Mr Jackson**.*

● **Narrator:** Every day Harry is bullied by Louis and his gang. They are making his life so miserable that Harry decides to go and tell an adult.

*Harry nervously walks up to **Mr Jackson** in the dining hall. The hall is filled with **children** talking and **Thomas** is standing on a table.*

● **Harry:** Umm…Mr Jackson?

● **Mr Jackson:** Thomas Clark, get down from that table before you hurt yourself! (*looks at **Harry***) Yes, what is it, Harry?

● **Harry:** Can I talk to you about something?

● **Mr Jackson:** Is it quick? (***Harry** nods*) OK, go on.

● **Harry:** It's about Louis and his gang. They're being nasty to me.

🟢 **Mr Jackson:** I'm sure they don't mean to be, Harry. Thomas, what did I say earlier? (*shouts*) GET DOWN!

🔵 **Harry:** But it happens everyday…

🟢 **Mr Jackson:** (*shouting*) THOMAS!

🔵 **Harry:** But…

Mr Jackson leaves Harry and walks over to Thomas.

🔴 **Narrator:** Harry realises Mr Jackson is too busy at the moment and he feels even more alone than ever. As he walks out of the dining hall, Harry hopes Louis and his gang won't spot him, but they do…

🟣 **Louis:** (*pointing*) There he is, quick, catch him!

Harry and the gang begin to run.

CHARACTERS IN THIS SCENE:

● Narrator ● Harry ● Mum ● Dad ● Millie

Mum, Dad and Millie are sitting around the breakfast table but Harry is not there.

🔴 **Narrator:** Louis has been at Harry's school for over a month and Louis and his gang are bullying Harry every day – in fact, the bullying is getting worse. They are making his life miserable, just as they said they would, and Harry does not know what to do. He is afraid.

🟢 **Mum:** *(calling from the bottom of the stairs)* Harry, breakfast is ready! You will be late for school if you don't hurry up.

🔵 **Harry:** *(calling down)* I'm not hungry.

🟠 **Millie:** *(looking shocked and drops her spoon back into her cereal bowl in surprise)* …But Harry is always hungry!

🟣 **Dad:** *(looking at Mum)* Let's go and check on him.

Mum and Dad exit the kitchen and enter Harry's bedroom.

🟢 **Mum:** What's wrong, Harry?

🔵 **Harry:** *(curled up in a ball and is hiding underneath the duvet covers)* I don't feel well. I can't go to school today. I'm really sick!

● **Mum**: (*feeling **Harry**'s forehead*) You don't feel hot and you look perfectly healthy. You don't want to miss out on all the things Ms Newton is going to teach you, do you?

● **Harry**: (*shouting*) I CAN'T!

● **Dad**: What's wrong, Harry? Why can't you go to school?

● **Harry**: Louis and his gang will be there! They hate me. I'd rather stay at home with you. (*sobbing*) Please don't make me go to school anymore.

● **Dad**: Harry, calm down. Now, tell us everything…

● **Harry**: (*sniffing*) It all started when Louis joined the school. I could tell he didn't like me from his very first day. And now it's just getting worse every day…

● **Narrator**: Harry starts to tell Mum and Dad everything. He tells them about the name calling, the rumours and lies the gang are spreading about him and about how he is made to feel as though he has no friends and that no one likes him.

● **Mum:** Harry, we can't let these bullies get away with this. It's important to stand up to them. Come now, we'll go in and talk to your teacher…together.

SCENE 6

CHARACTERS IN THIS SCENE:
● **Narrator** ● **Harry** ● **Mum** ● **Ms Newton**

Harry and his mum are in the classroom talking to Ms Newton.

● **Harry:** Louis and his gang are horrible to me every day. I don't want to come to school anymore.

● **Ms Newton:** Why didn't you tell anyone about this sooner, Harry?

● **Harry:** Louis said that if I told anyone he would spread more rumours about me. He said everyone would believe him and that no one would be my friend.

● **Mum:** Harry, you must tell Ms Newton everything. That way she can help you sort this out.

● **Narrator:** By the end of an hour, Ms Newton had written a full page of notes about the bullying.

Ms Newton looks down at her notes. Pause whilst she considers what to do.

🔴 **Ms Newton:** (*looking at* **Harry**) Harry, you must understand that nobody has the right to make you feel afraid of them. Bullies have no place at this school. Now, I will speak to Louis about this but you must promise me that if this happens again, you come straight to me or your mum.

🔵 **Harry**: (*sniffing but looking happier*) OK.

🔴 **Narrator:** Harry begins to realise that there are people who will take his troubles seriously. He now knows that if the first person you tell doesn't listen to you, you must find someone who will.

CHARACTERS IN THIS SCENE:

● Narrator ● Louis ● Ms Newton ● Faisal ● Lily
● Alfie ● Extras – *children outside the classroom*

*Ms Newton calls **Louis** into the classroom. **Louis** and his **gang** are chatting outside in the playground.*

● **Ms Newton:** Can I have a quick word, Louis?

● **Extras:** Ooooh, you're in trouble, Louis! What have you done now?

*Ms Newton and **Louis** enter the classroom and sit down.*

● **Ms Newton:** Louis, I need to talk to you about something very serious and upsetting. Several people have noticed some very unkind things happening in our school recently. What can you tell me about this?

● **Louis:** *(fidgeting and looking uneasy)* Ummm…nothing, Ms Newton. I don't know what you mean.

● **Ms Newton:** Well, can you tell me what has been going on between you and Harry?

● **Louis:** *(defensively)* Nothing, just ask Faisal or Lily!

Ms Newton: I'm asking you, Louis. Lying will only get you into more trouble. I think you know that bullying is not acceptable.

Louis: But it's not just me. Alfie, Lily and Faisal have been nasty, too!

● **Ms Newton:** From what I understand, Louis, they left Harry alone until you persuaded them to join in with your bullying. You need to accept some of the responsibility here.

● **Narrator:** Ms Newton speaks to Louis for more than half an hour. By the end of their time together, she understands more about the reasons behind Louis' bullying and thinks she can find a way to help both Harry and Louis.

● **Louis:** *(looking miserable)* I don't think I really thought about how my actions would make Harry feel, Ms Newton, honestly I didn't. I have been so caught up in my own problems at home.

● **Narrator:** It turns out that Louis has been miserable at home. His mum is always so busy with the new baby and his dad is away in the Army. Louis has been taking out his anger and loneliness on Harry.

● **Ms Newton:** I believe you, Louis. Now it is your chance to make it up to Harry. He deserves to feel wanted at school but you have made him feel just as alone here as you feel at home. Harry could be a friend to you and someone you turn to when you feel lonely.

● **Louis:** I'll think about how I can put this right, Ms Newton, I promise.

SCENE 8

CHARACTERS IN THIS SCENE:
● Narrator ● Harry ● Mum ● Dad ● Millie

HAPPY BIRTHDAY!

Harry, *Mum*, *Dad* and *Millie* are in the house. It is *Harry*'s birthday.

🟢 **Mum:** Let's have a party to celebrate your birthday, Harry! You can invite all your friends from school.

🔵 **Harry:** *(worrying)* But what if no one comes? Louis might tell them all to stay away from me!

🟠 **Millie:** Well, why don't you invite Louis, too? He hasn't been horrible to you at school ever since you spoke to Ms Newton about the bullying. Maybe he knows he was wrong and would like to be your friend now.

🔵 **Harry:** *(thinking)* Maybe…

🟠 **Millie:** I think Harry and Dad should go over to Louis' house right now and invite Louis to the party.

🟣 **Dad:** *(looks at **Harry**)* Shall we, Harry?

🔵 **Harry:** *(nervously)* OK.

SCENE 9

CHARACTERS IN THIS SCENE:
● Narrator ● Harry ● Dad ● Louis
● Mrs Hastings

Harry and *Dad* knock on the front door of *Louis'* home.

● **Mrs Hastings:** *(off stage)* Can you get the door, Louis? I need to bath the baby. I won't be long.

Louis opens the door to find *Harry* and his *dad* on the doorstep.

● **Harry:** Hi, Louis, this is my dad. *(nervously points to his dad)* I just… I was wondering if you wanted to come to my birthday party on Saturday?

● **Louis:** *(breaking into a huge grin)* That would be amazing, Harry, thanks! Actually, what are you doing now? Do you want to play computer games with me?

● **Harry**: That sounds cool! *(grins at his dad)* Can I, Dad?

● **Dad:** Of course, Harry. Louis, tell your mum I'll pick Harry up at 4 o'clock.

Harry enters the house. When the door closes, **Dad** can hear laughter as he walks away.

● **Narrator:** Harry feels much happier than he has in a long time. He is no longer lonely at school and often goes round to play at Louis' house. Louis has learnt that by saying nice things and making other people feel good about themselves he feels better, too. And he has made a new friend in Harry.

The End

Remember, bullying is always cruel and no one deserves to be bullied, it should always be stopped. Telling someone you trust is the first step in beating the bullies. If you are a bully, think about why you bully people. Can you talk to someone about your problems, so that they can help you?

If you or anyone you know is a target of bullying, there are people and places you can contact for advice:

Kidscape: www.kidscape.org.uk
A registered charity which provides books, videos, teaching packs and leaflets on how to deal with bullying.

Anti-Bullying Campaign: www.bullying.co.uk
Offers practical information and advice to young people and their parents about bullying.

First published in 2011 by Wayland

Copyright © Wayland 2011

Wayland
338 Euston Road
London
NW1 3BH

Wayland Australia
Level 17/207 Kent Street
Sydney NSW 2000

All rights reserved.

Editor: Katie Woolley
Designer: Elaine Wilkinson
Illustrator: Sophie Keen
Consultant: Claude Knights, Kidscape

British Library Cataloguing in
Publication Data
Powell, Jenny.
 Stop bullying me!. -- (Putting on
 a play)
 1. Bullying--Juvenile drama.
 I. Title II. Series
 822.9'2-dc22

ISBN: 978 0 7502 6549 2

Printed in China

Wayland is a division of Hachette
Children's Books, an Hachette
UK company.
www.hachette.co.uk